Management –

Things Your Mother Never Told You
2nd Edition

Kathy Pourmehr

Acknowledgement

Thanks to my wonderful husband, Faramarz, for his constant support!

Table of Contents

Introduction

How to Use this Book

The intent of this book is to give you a heads up on how to avoid "gotchas" as a manager. It can also be a refresher on how to progress in your career as a manager, as well as how to stay out of trouble as a manager. This is an easy to read, short book, that touches on the topics of management that I feel are important. This book is not filled with quotes or statistics from the management experts. You can get those from reading one of the many famous books published by the management gurus. Instead, this book is filled with practical advice on things you will encounter throughout your career as a manager. I expect that you will read this and think to yourself, "Huh, I've had that happen to me." Even though I have held every position of management (excluding at the Chief level), I always find it useful to attend a conference and here about other managers' experiences. I always find a way to apply their experiences to my situations, and use their ideas to improve my performance. Many times, I nod in agreement, knowing that I had encountered a similar situation and handled it the exact same way. Other times I make note of their actions and results, with the intent of adding them to my repertoire of things to do to be a good manager. It is my intent with this book to either get your nod of agreement, or get your acknowledgement that my thoughts will help you through a difficult situation.

Note that this book is not intended to help you manage your staff better, although it does touch on this throughout. It is really intended to help you survive and thrive as a manager. I have been continuously promoted as a result of following this advice. It is time to share this with you.

Why am I Writing this Book

You go to high school and get a diploma. You go to college and get a degree. During the many years of education, what type of information is shared with you to prepare you for the "real world?" How many of your teachers or professors held management positions in a business? How much knowledge do they have based on actual experience managing a business, managing employees, or, even, managing their own careers? Did any of your teachers discuss politics? Not Democratic or Republican politics, rather, corporate politics. What about your mother or father? Did they ever sit you down to have a talk about a career in management, or how to deal with corporate politics? If you grew up and were educated in the same manner as me, the answer to all of the above questions is a resounding "No!"

In fact, I didn't even realize that I would encounter a different set of issues the further up the career ladder I moved until they hit me in the face! I can say with confidence that I was not mentally prepared for what was to come. As a result, and in an attempt to help others so that they can be somewhat prepared, I am writing this book.

We have all been taught to learn from others' mistakes. There is no reason to repeat bad history if it can be helped. Not only that, this book is intended to help you succeed in management. It is always nice to be able to take on a new role and hit the ground running. Reading this book will help you do just that. You will know how to impress from the beginning, be productive from the start. You will learn how to recognize the key players and which players to steer clear of. You will recognize the traps before you fall prey to them.

As a manager, you will have sleepless nights, something I have not found a way to avoid. Hopefully, these can be minimized. This is something that goes along with the territory. You need to make tough decisions that will affect you, your employees, and your business. Some of these decisions are only in the best interest of the business, having a negative impact on your employees and you. You could be asked to set aside your own personal feelings, as there could be a conflict between your feelings and the needs of the business.

At times, you may feel unqualified for the job you have been given. Give yourself time. It takes time to become productive when starting a new job. I allow myself six months to become comfortable and effective in a new job. During this time, I rely on my staff to help with the decision making. It also takes time to work through problems. Be somewhat patient with yourself, however, note that management will not tolerate too much time without producing results.

Some individuals are just not cut out for management. The decision to put these individuals into positions where they are likely to fail is a shortcoming of management.

It is my intent by writing this book to help you avoid the pitfalls of management. If you cannot avoid the pitfalls, at a minimum, you will be aware that the pitfalls exist and will have some notion of how to handle them. Being prepared is half of the battle. No surprises! Simply knowing that obstacles will be thrown in your path gives you an awareness that not everyone has. While being part of the management team should give you a level of influence which could help you direct your destiny, it also places you in an untrusted category. Employees have a tendency to not trust management. Part of your challenge will be to gain that trust, leading to a productive environment in which employees will contribute to your success.

This is a large order to fill: help you succeed as a manager, prevent the pitfalls that lead to management downfalls, maintain a productive organization, make the tough decisions to keep the business successful, manage your boss while managing your employees, recognize the traps, make your business profitable, maintain a delighted customer base, deliver on your commitments, master corporate politics, and deal with peer competition, all while ensuring a successful career for yourself. It is all possible. I have been through all of this, and have always ended up on top. It has been my goal to educate others in these ways to help them be as successful as I have been, hence, the reason for writing this book.

Intended Audience

This book is intended for those considering management as part of their career plan. It is also intended for those struggling in management. It is never too late to step back, make changes to your approach, and go forward, turning a struggle into a success. In fact, much of what I have learned over the years has been the result of a problem. I have had to figure out the strategy and direction without the benefit of such a book. I have definitely learned from my mistakes.

One more member of the audience is that individual planning a fresh start in a new management position. Take what you learned from your last position, read this book, and apply both to your new position. In addition to manager wannabe's, this book can help employees understand how managers think, why they make the decisions they make.

Even though I have held management positions ranging from Project Manager through President, I have always been searching for a "Management 101" book to remind me of what it takes to succeed. I never considered myself to be so successful that I didn't need help, either in the form of a reference book, in the form of a discussion with a mentor, through research on the internet, or even a chat with my manager. Therefore, this book could also be beneficial to experienced managers as well. It can be considered a reference tool, simply a reminder of what to do or how to do it.

My Qualifications

By now, you are probably wondering what are my qualifications to write this book. I have held management positions for over 15 years, starting out as a junior IT Project Manager, moving into a General Manager position of an IT company, then a Development Manager position leading a software development organization, a Director of IT Customer Service, Vice President of Operations, Vice President of Systems Integration, President of the Southeast Region of an IT Consulting firm, Director of Operations Management, Director of Consulting, and, finally, Director of Enterprise Applications. I have a Bachelor's Degree in Business Administration, Computer Information Systems, a Master's Degree in Business Administration, and a Doctorate in Business Administration. I also have an Executive Diploma in Quality Management, and have professional American Society for Quality certification as a Manager of Quality/Organizational Excellence and as a Software Quality Engineer.

Over the years, I have mastered the skill of management. Each challenge became a new game. In almost all cases, I obtained my preferred outcome. I have been offered every job I have ever interviewed for. In certain companies, I was the sole management survivor in merger after merger after acquisition. I have learned which jobs I like and I can excel in versus which jobs I am no good at. I have learned how to become a member of the inner circle. I have also learned that I am not happy unless I am a member of the inner circle. I have been paid the ultimate compliment, being told that I am the first and only manager that actually taught someone something. Stepping into a new management position, managing managers who wanted my job, winning over a pre-existing management team, are all challenging and rewarding. I have done this many, many times, and have succeeded in almost all instances.

I have encountered many different situations, all of which contributed to my ability to be a more effective manager. These situations include peers competing for my position, unhappy customers, new bosses, unhappy managers, unhappy employees, businesses in trouble, layoffs, mergers, acquisitions, diversity, global teams, cross functional teams, etc. I can't think of any management problem that I have not been part of. I have hired, fired, trained, fought, schemed, mentored, ran businesses, developed business, shut down businesses, promoted deserving employees, demoted deserving employees, and the list goes on.

Management 101

What is Management?

The Merriam-Webster definition of Management is:

> **The act or art of <u>managing</u> : the conducting or supervising of something (as a business).[1]**

Businessdictionary.com defines management as:

> **Organization and coordination of the activities of an enterprise in accordance with certain policies and in achievement of clearly defined objectives. Management is often included as a factor of production along with machines, materials, and money. According to the management guru Peter Drucker (1909-2005), the basic task of a management is twofold: marketing and innovation. Practice of modern management owes its origin to the 16th century enquiry into low-efficiency and failures of certain enterprises, conducted by the English statesman Sir Thomas More (1478-1535).[2]**

I view management as being responsible for Planning,

Organizing, Directing, and Controlling. When an individual

13

takes on a management role, they must plan the direction of the business and organization, they must then organize to execute the plan. Organizing includes hiring and positioning the staff in order to carry out the plan. The manager must then direct the organization to execute the plan. Sometimes directing requires training, it often requires significant communication, it requires tracking progress against the plan, keeping the train on the tracks and moving in the right direction. Controlling requires steering the organization to keep it on track. If the performance of the organization starts to veer from the plan, it is the manager's job to step back, take a look at what is causing the deviation, fix the cause of variation, and get the organization back on track.

A manager is responsible for establishing goals and objectives for the organization. The plan for the organization is based on these goals and objectives. The plan must be supportive of the goals and objectives. These goals and objectives must be documented and shared with the entire organization. They must not be in conflict with your manager's or your peers' goals and objectives. The objectives must be measurable and attainable. One measurement of successful management is the capability of the organization to achieve its objectives. The objectives should be set based on the pressing issues of the organization that need to be addressed. The objectives should be aggressive, yet achievable. Aggressive objectives require team members to go above and beyond. The manager needs to recognize whether they can succeed in the achievement of the objectives, or fail. If failure is eminent, the objectives are too aggressive. When the team fails, so does the manager. Management cannot achieve the objectives without the backing, support, and efforts of the entire organization. Therefore, a good manager celebrates the achievement of the objectives with the entire organization. A good manager touts the successes of the organization at every opportunity. Reaching the role of management means setting aside shyness and humbleness.

Your success as a manager requires that you advertise your successes. They will be noticed but forgotten as time goes by. Therefore, constant reminders prove valuable. A good manager will constantly seek accolades for his organization. You must constantly present progress in achieving objectives, showing your actual measurements versus the planned measurements. The team will appreciate the constant recognition, your boss will appreciate the constant reminders, helping you, as the manager, gain respect as a good manager.

A manager is responsible for evaluating the performance of each member of the organization. Your boss is responsible for evaluating your performance. Performance evaluations are based on the objectives. Achieving the objectives leads to a good performance evaluation. A good performance evaluation leads to pay raises and promotions.

There is an administrative side to management. Part of this was already mentioned in the form of performance evaluations. Human Resources (HR) sets processes that must be followed in support of the employees. Every employee deserves feedback on his performance. This could be either positive or negative feedback. Presenting positive feedback is easy and rewarding. Presenting negative feedback is difficult, uneasy, and necessary. A successful manager has an organization full of over-achievers. It is the responsibility of a good manager to deal with the under-achievers. Under-achievers cause harm to the remainder of the organization, especially the over-achievers. It is not fair to those working many hours to make the business successful to have some who arrive late, leave early, and don't get their jobs done. It is the job of the manager to prevent these differences. Under-achievers pull down the organization, causing over-achievers to re-think their responsibilities. If under-achievers get rewarded for poor performance equal to over-achievers, why should anyone be willing to sacrifice their personal lives for their jobs.

In addition to performance evaluations, managers are responsible for setting and following budgets, performing salary administration, assisting employees with their career plans, mentoring more junior managers, etc.

Some individuals are not cut out for management. They are not interested in the administrative side of management. They are not comfortable dealing with employee performance issues. They cannot communicate as effectively as is necessary to articulate the progress of the organization. Once someone reaches the rank of management, their hands-on ability diminishes, making them less marketable in their field of expertise. Instead, they become experts in managing hands-on organizations. An effective manager can contribute to the technical operations of the team due to his experience in having done what they do. While you may no longer be hands-on, you will still be involved in the technical direction of the organization.

So, what is management? It is doing everything necessary to make the organization successful. It is work, but it is rewarding work. It is setting objectives, achieving objectives, and getting credit for a job well done! It is helping other individuals achieve their career goals. It is being told that you were their inspiration. Managing is controlling the direction of a business, and steering the organization to succeed. Management is contributing to the profitability of a company, and being given credit for the contribution.

What is Bad Management?

Bad management is allowing an organization to fail. Not setting objectives leads to failure. The organization needs to know what they are striving to achieve. The success of the organization is measured based on their ability to achieve their objectives. If no objectives are set, the organization does not work towards a common goal. Chaos causes failure. Lack of goals and objectives causes chaos.

A bad manager does not give feedback to employees. The employees don't know whether they are performing according to expectations or not. The feedback, whether positive or negative, is needed to let employees know how they are doing. Bad management doesn't care about the performance of the employees. This leads to employee turnover, which leads to chaos.

Bad management does not follow processes. Processes are key to help employees do their jobs. They help ensure consistency in what employees do and how they do it.

A bad manager does not actively participate in budgeting. Setting a valid budget helps the employees to do their jobs. A good budget allows the purchase of necessary technology, scheduling necessary training, celebrating successes. Lack of budget tracking prevents future funds to be awarded. If a manager cannot articulate the budget needs of the organization, the organization will lose out in receiving necessary funds.

A bad manager makes decisions purely based on costs, not understanding the impact to the business as a result. He will choose a cheaper solution which will make him look good as a result of costs savings. However, it will come back to haunt the company later. That manager, the one who was given accolades for saving the company money, will probably not

be around to suffer the consequences of his bad decisions.

A bad manager does not have the trust of upper

management. Upper management's trust is needed in order

to know the plans of the business. This gives a manager

insight into job opportunities for the employees of the

organization. It also ensures that the manager sets objectives

supportive of the success of the business. A manager can

only gain "insider information" if he has the trust of upper

management. Being part of the planning process for the

future of the business is very important to an individual in a

management role. If you are excluded from this process, you

cannot ensure your future role.

What is Good Management?

A good manager knows the future of the business. He is made aware of the future by being part of the inner circle. The senior management team confides in those managers believed to be leaders at their level. They will ask the high performing managers for their opinions on the plans for the business. This will give you the opportunity to make sure you have a chair when the music stops playing. When given a preview of the future plans, you will be able to establish your position based on your knowledge of the organization, how upper management views your value, and based on your experiences and qualifications.

Once you have been able to establish your future, you then have the opportunity to build an organization that will make you successful. The key to success as a manager is to surround yourself with strong, loyal players. You need a team that will go to bat for you. A team that will vouch for your abilities. Getting first pick of the players gives you the opportunity to build that strong, supportive organization that you will come to rely on. Your team can make or break you. A series of complaints from your team members will cause upper management to question your qualifications. If, however, you have a supportive team, a team that is in agreement with your plans and direction, the complaints will be few and far between. It is impossible to please everyone, therefore, you must expect some unhappiness among the troops. However, if you include them in your planning, you will gain their buy-in, leading to gaining their support. Those who agree with your plans will help you succeed.

Good management includes the team in the planning. If they are involved, they will be supportive. In order to be able to delegate effectively, the team leaders need to see the big picture. Including them in the planning will give them this opportunity. They will then stop you from making a mistake if they see that you are straying from the plan. There are times, however, when you simply cannot share with them the plan. They will understand, however, once the plan is rolled out and announced. Those that you select to be the leaders know that you are the manager for a reason, that there are times when you have been asked by your manager to not share the information presented to you. When asked by your manager to hold something in confidence, it is extremely important that you honor that request! If you divulge the information and your manager is made aware of this, you will lose your position in the inner circle—probably one of the worst situations you could encounter as a manager. You may even lose your job!

I am a strong believer of a little downtime for the team once in a while. The team works hard to succeed and make you a success, they deserve some fun time as a team as well. Team outings and team-building activities are always fun and always appreciated by everyone.

A good manager is aligned with HR. HR is extremely important to you as a manager. They will keep you out of trouble legally. They will tout your abilities as a manager to upper management. HR surveys employees for their satisfaction working for the company. Most of the time, employees have the opportunity to enter free text comments in these surveys. It is your job to make these employees happy at the workplace leading to positive comments in these surveys. When it is necessary to take action for or against an employee, HR will help you along the way, ensuring you are following the processes. If done correctly, and if an employee takes legal action against the company for a supposed wrong doing, you will be protected. HR can keep you out of HR jail. In addition, if you become a candidate for promotion, HR could be the deciding factor between you and your competition.

A good manager works closely with the Finance Department. It is important to establish a valid, realistic budget and follow it. It is also important to participate in business development. Contributing to the bottom line of the business is a responsibility of a manager. A good manager can help plan revenue streams and control costs. A good manager knows the plans of his customers and can forecast the services they will purchase in the future. Management is responsible for ensuring all potential expenses are included in the budget and that actual expenses do not exceed planned expenses. Staying within budget is a performance measurement for management. A good manager spends his budget and helps develop new business opportunities. In addition, a good manager keeps his eyes on the competition. The ultimate goal is to keep one step ahead of the competition. Winning the customers before the competition does. If your customers are only internal customers, your goal is to give them what they want, when they want it. You need to provide the best service possible, otherwise, even your internal customers can opt to go outside of the business and seek service elsewhere.

A manager who wants to get ahead volunteers to take on more. This includes taking on the difficult tasks that nobody else will take on. One caveat to this – you need to be certain you can get it done. If you fail at delivery, you will not be given this opportunity again. Once you reach the ranks of management, you are given one shot to fail. You can't have the attitude of "that's not my job." Upper management always appreciates someone willing to do what is needed to make the business successful. It is very rewarding to take on what appears to be an impossible task, find a solution to the problem, and implement the solution. It is important that you believe that you are responsible for the success of the business and that there is nothing that you won't take on to ensure this success. In many instances, someone will tell you that that is not your job, however, if it was not being addressed by anyone else, then it becomes your job. Your peers will become very insecure when you start to take on tasks that maybe they should have been handling. In my opinion, that is their problem. If the work needs to get done and you know what or how to do it, get it done! Yes, you need to be a team player and get along with your peers. However, it should be your goal to be looked at as the leader at your level, setting an example for your peers.

A good manager is able to make quick assessments and take action quickly. Sometimes, if an action looks like it is not going to result in the preferred outcome, it is necessary to stop and adjust the plan, and then continue. A good manager recognizes that something is not working and takes steps to get back on the right track. A good manager is not afraid to stop and say "this isn't working." It is important to show quick progress. Choose those things that can be completed quickly and successfully, and get those done first.

A good manager does not admit to knowing everything. If you don't understand something, it is important to speak up and ask for clarification. I never pretend to be an expert in all areas. I rely on my management team to be experts in their areas, and to keep me educated in the direction they are going. I am not too shy to ask "stupid" questions. I know that my questions are not stupid, and I ask them in order to do my job better. I feel that I need to be able to understand and explain everything we are doing as an organization. Sometimes that means that my team needs to educate me. I also do a great deal of research myself to keep up. Technology is progressing at a rapid pace and I need to keep up with what we are doing as a business to meet the needs of our customers. As a result, I ask a lot of questions. Regardless, I do have a strong technical background which allows me to assist my organization to succeed. While I was trained in older technology, I still have a technical background and can still apply my skills to today's technology. My teams feel comfortable discussing technical issues with me and seeking my advice on how to proceed. They appreciate being able to come to me for these discussions.

So, as a good manager, you have looked out for the employees, you have worked closely with HR, and you have aligned yourself with Finance. Upper management thinks you are a key player. Now, what do you do with all of this? You use it to promote yourself! You take every opportunity to brag about your successes! You remind your boss of these successes in your performance self-appraisal. You present your successes in weekly staff meetings. You document your successes in weekly status reports to upper management.

You will get recognition, as will your team. It is a win-win

situation for everyone associated with you!

Managing Employees

How to Deal With Bad Employees

Underperforming employees are a problem for you and your organization. They cause morale issues throughout the team. Those employees working hard to be successful will think it unfair when an underperforming employee gets an annual raise, or even keeps his job. It is up to you, as the manager, to deal with this problem head on. HR will require that poor performance be properly documented. If this employee reports directly to you, it is your job to complete this documentation. If, however, this employee reports to one of your direct reports, it is the job of the direct report to complete the documentation. Each instance of poor performance must be documented. It is my opinion that if the employee is at a Director or above level, he does not get the privilege of being put on a Performance Improvement

Plan (PIP). Instead, he gets the unfortunate destiny of being fired. Directors are expected to perform at above average levels. That is how they became a Director in the first place. All other employees deserve the chance to fix their performance problems.

If the employee is below a Director level, he should be put on a PIP. I give problem employees one opportunity to miss the objectives in a PIP. After the second failure, they are fired. When reviewing this plan with the problematic employee, you need to be very clear about your expectations of him achieving the plan, with no exceptions. The employee needs to understand that missing an objective of the plan is cause for termination. It is important that the PIP be clear, with clearly outlined expected deliverables along with delivery dates. The deliverables cannot be dependent on someone else's work. The employee must be able to complete the deliverables independent of anyone or anything. If the employee misses a deliverable as a result of someone else's involvement, and, you agree that that could not be helped, then the miss cannot count against the employee. A PIP takes a lot of time and work on the part of management. It is important to assess the potential value the employee can have to the organization. It the employee is deemed valuable, then the effort may be worth it. If, however, the employee is not worth the effort, it may be worthwhile to have a direct talk with the employee and sway them to leave voluntarily.

A manager cannot afford to have feelings when dealing with performance issues. The employee needs to be told that he is a performance issue. The employee deserves specific examples of how he is not measuring up. In many instances, I have had employees resign on their own, finding jobs that they are better suited for, without the need for personnel action. This is always the best outcome when performance issues arise. Otherwise, you may have to deal with legal ramifications of firing an employee. They may claim discrimination as the cause of their firing. A claim of discrimination could be based on age, gender, nationality, race, or religion. As a result of this possibility, it is important to work closely with HR to ensure the proper procedure is followed, that all t's are crossed and i's are dotted. If you have covered all of your bases and have sufficient, clear documentation to show performance issues, you don't need to worry about possible legal action.

The one thing that is most important when dealing with performance issues is to be clear and direct. Ignoring the problem makes matters worse, and the problem won't go away on its own. This may be difficult for some to handle; however, to be a good manager, it is important to be able to address the tough issues without hesitation. It works to your advantage to show that you are not afraid to deal with problems. You gain the respect of your team, as well as that of upper management.

I have grown thick skin over the years. I have learned to set aside my feelings when at work, to make my decisions based on logic. This has been key to my success as a manager. I have worked with managers who "care" about their employees, to the extent that they appear to go to bat for anyone on their team, whether deserving or not. After a couple times of defending undeserving employees, the manager loses credibility as an effective manager. If you are going to defend an employee, make sure that it is for a worthy cause. Also, make sure that the employee is worthy of the defense. Otherwise, you are putting your own reputation on the line.

I have had instances where I knew an employee was doing a much better job than understood by upper management. I was also aware of the potential harm to the business if that employee quit or was fired. Under these circumstances, I was willing to defend an employee to upper management. While upper management did not agree to the value of the employee, I was able to maintain the employee and award him a much deserved pay raise without jeopardizing my own standing in the eyes of upper management. I could accomplish this by presenting the facts. The facts included accomplishments on the part of the employee, as well as presenting the impact to the organization if the employee was gone. I was successful in my argument by having the facts and being able to present them setting all emotions aside. I would only defend an employee like this if I felt it absolutely necessary. I do not do this often. This activity is reserved for truly deserving employees and circumstances that I believe warrant me putting my reputation on the line.

Usually, there is more work than can be finished by the existing employee base. As a result, it is very important that your team be staffed by high performers. It is a good idea to rank your employees on an annual basis. Those employees falling in the lower 10 percent should either improve their performance or be terminated. Eventually, it becomes very difficult to draw the line at 10 percent, however, when comparing employees against each other, there is always a lower 10 percent. Performance is one factor to be used when making this decision. Attitude, which, technically, is part of performance, is also to be considered. Employees who can do the work, but complain the entire time, become burdensome to the rest of the organization. Peers of these employees are not in a position to do anything about this, other than to try to ignore the complaints. You, as a manager, are responsible for dealing with this situation. I am a true believer of the philosophy that anyone can be replaced! This philosophy has helped me deal with some potentially valuable employees with bad attitudes. Knowing that I can find a replacement, someone who can do the work and have a good attitude about it, makes it easier to deal with these troublesome employees. Yes, it may take a little time, however, it will be worth it in the long run! Some upper management teams require ranking employees on an annual basis. It is not a good idea to tell upper management that all of your employees are perfect and nobody deserves to fall below the 10 percent line. They will think that you are not an objective manager. Therefore, bite the bullet and draw the line. It is not in your best interest to have someone else draw that line for you!

It is important to be direct when dealing with employee issues. Beating around the bush won't get the issue resolved. You need to set aside your emotions and deal with the issue in a serious manner. Don't be shy, don't be nervous, don't be emotional, be direct and confident. Remember that by taking care of poor performing employees, you are helping the entire organization, and helping yourself!

How to Deal With Good Employees

Dealing with good employees is much easier than dealing with bad employees. Good employees want a career path. They want to know what the future holds for them. It is important that you work closely with HR to ensure such a career path exists. Remember that there needs to be two different branches to the career path – technical and management. Some employees don't want to join the ranks of management. They prefer to be individual contributors, continuing to excel technically. The salaries and authority need to be equal between the two paths, regardless of which branch is followed. In other words, a Staff Engineer should be ranked equal to a Manager, both in salary and authority, the difference being that a Staff Engineer is expected to stay current with technology, researching newer and better ways to do things, while a Manager is expected to handle the day-to-day administrative tasks of managing a team.

Good employees need to be recognized. Their accomplishments should be shared with the entire organization and they should be given credit for a job well done. Hopefully, this will motivate the remaining employee base to do a better job, to go above and beyond. I have done many different things to recognize good work, stemming from financial bonuses, higher pay raises, restaurant gift cards, days off, movie tickets, etc. The intent of these gifts is to give the employee an opportunity to celebrate their successes with someone other than the team members they work with. The objective of these rewards is for the employee to spend time with family or friends, to take a small break from a stressful working environment. This helps them recharge and get ready for the next challenge.

Good employees deserve raving performance evaluations. Even though they may seem perfect due to their ability to get the work done, it is still important to find areas needing improvement, no matter how small they may be. Upper management expects that everyone can improve somewhere, somehow. It is up to you to make sure you point out these areas, otherwise, upper management will question your objectivity as a manager. Sometimes you have to really search for these opportunities for improvement. In fact, sometimes you need to discuss this with the employee to get their thoughts on the subject. The topic of "what do you need to do to improve" can be approached lightheartedly, especially when you need to ask the employee to help figure this out. The two of you will have a good laugh over the conversation, however, it is important that this be covered in the employee's performance evaluation.

Good employees look for career advancement. If you want to keep them on your team, you need to give them these advancement opportunities. Again, working with HR will help you with this dilemma. Positions for advancement may not be readily available within your organization. It is your job to figure out how to create these positions, justifying the budget and the return on investment. In this case, the return on investment is based on not needing to spend time or money recruiting to hire a replacement if the employee would decide to leave the company due to lack of advancement opportunities. Also, the workload will suffer if the employee leaves, including the ramp up time for a new employee. This loss of work needs to be given a dollar value. You need to consider every impact to the business as a result of losing a valuable employee, and always put it in terms of dollars. Add them all together and get the total cost of losing this valuable employee. Management pays attention to dollars.

Good employees want to be part of the planning team. They take an interest in the future of the organization and the business. They want to be included. It is a good idea to have skip-level meetings with these employees. A skip-level meeting is one in which their direct manager is not invited, only you and the employees. These meetings give the employees an opportunity to speak up without repercussions. They will say things to you that they are not comfortable saying to their manager. It is important that these meetings do not turn into complaint and whining sessions. If the whining begins, you need to redirect the discussion towards a more productive topic. In fact, you need to open every meeting with the comment that the intent of the meeting is to learn and improve, not to whine and complain. The intent of these meetings is for actions to come out of them leading to a better work environment. Sometimes these meetings generate actions for the management team under you. Sometimes they generate actions for you. If you are going to hold such meetings, you need to show that you are making changes as a result of the input you receive. Otherwise, employees will attend without speaking up, thinking that this is just another management fad.

Most companies these days have an "open door policy." This means that any employee can go into any office and meet with anybody. I have had numerous discussions with managers reporting to me regarding the behavior of their employees. More immature employees abuse this policy, using it to whine and complain about issues that, while they feel are important, are not going to be addressed by anyone given the priorities of the business. When an employee does this, they are hurting themselves, they are hurting their manager, and they are hurting you. This can be prevented by proper coaching of these employees. Managers know who they are. Managers need to have one-on-one discussions with these employees to stop them from escalating their concerns unnecessarily.

An "open door policy" allows your employees to meet directly with your manager. Sometimes your manager will give them work assignments that you are unaware of. When this happens, you need to meet with your manager and remind him that you cannot manage effectively and help him with his objectives if you are unaware of the assignments he is giving your employees. At times, employees begin to feel comfortable going directly to your manager, especially if your manager makes himself available at their request. This could lead to an environment where employees feel overly comfortable confronting senior management. When this happens, I have seen a lack of respect shown towards people of authority. I grew up in industry with the understanding that each level of authority gets a different level of respect. A CIO should never be confronted directly by a junior engineer!

Managing Customers

What is a Customer?

Customers can be internal or external. Internal customers are those that depend on the work you do so that they can do their work, and they work for the same company you work for. An example of an internal customer would be the HR Department, assuming they are using a software application that you are responsible for supporting. They can pay for your services either through budget allocations, or you could be allocated a budget in which you are responsible for supporting all of your internal customers. If an internal customer needs additional services, services that were not budgeted for, it is the customer's responsibility to help you acquire the necessary budget to proceed. Merriam-Webster.com defines a Customer as:

one that purchases a commodity or service [3]

External customers pay for your services. Their payments fund your organization. If they want additional services, it is your responsibility to develop a pricing model and deliver a quote to them within a committed period of time. Your goal is to provide the best pricing possible while still generating a target profit.

How to Manage Your Customers

The better you service your customers, the greater your success as a manager. Sometimes you need to make a commitment to a customer without conferring with your team first. In these cases, you need to pull the organization together, explain the commitment, and then develop a plan to deliver. Missing deliverables to customers is career limiting, especially if the missed deliverable has a negative impact on the financials of the business. Meeting or beating deliverable commitments will do nothing but help you with your career plans. You know you have succeeded when your customers welcome you in and treat you as a partner. At this point in a customer relationship, they will share with you their budgets and plan, allowing you to put together a profitable plan for your business. An ongoing revenue stream is always preferred. A manager that can generate an ongoing revenue stream is considered a successful manager.

A key to success is to figure out how to give the customer what he wants. Sometimes it is necessary to give something away with the understanding that the customer will appreciate it so much that they will purchase services from you in the future. It is important to maintain an excellent working relationship with your customers. If they have a concern, you want them to call you, not your manager! They will call you if they believe you have the ability to take care of their issue. If they feel you are not able or not empowered, they will call your manager. The worst meetings I have ever had in my manager's office were those when a customer escalated an issue, not calling me first! Your team members will not all recognize the value of a satisfied customer and may not always understand the decisions you make in order to keep a customer happy. You can try to educate your employees on why you make the decisions you make, but they will not all agree, regardless of the reasoning. Therefore, don't expect them to always be on board when you need them to put in the extra hours to fix something that appears to be trivial.

Keeping customers happy allows you to keep your job. Unhappy customers will get you fired. That probably sounds pretty black and white, however, it is a fact! As I had written in a previous section, customers were key to getting me promoted and key to getting my colleague fired.

One compliment paid to me by one of my managers is that I deliver. Deliver, in this case, is referring to keeping customers happy. I make it a point to meet with my customers on a regular basis. I listen to their needs, I offer them hope, and I give them commitments. I then follow up on those commitments, communicating progress frequently. While I have missed commitments once in a while, it was usually due to circumstances beyond my control, mostly due to dependencies on my peer's organization. In those cases, I expected my peer to explain to the customer why we missed a delivery. If my organization was responsible for a missed delivery, I was the one to deliver the bad news. However, when I did have to deliver such a message, I did it with regret. My customers always knew that I worked for them.

At times, we had teams located at customer sites. They were dedicated teams charged with providing dedicated support. The challenge in this situation is that the team members start to think and act like the customer. While that is good in the eyes of the customer, it can be detrimental to your business. When the support teams don't get something from the central team, they start to badmouth the central team. Their comments are overheard by the customer. At times, I have had to bring team members back into the central team to give them a reminder of who pays their salary. It is hard enough to do a job to keep a customer happy, it becomes even harder when your own team starts to talk badly about the work you are doing within earshot of the customer! It is understandable how this can happen. The on-site team is trying to deliver for the customer and they are dependent on the central team to deliver solutions in a timely manner. If the solution doesn't arrive as expected, the on-site team takes the blame. If this becomes a regular occurrence, the on-site team shifts the blame to the central team, relieving them of the responsibility. The customer then begins to think we have no control over what we are doing or how we are doing it. In all cases, the customer's business has relied on our products to keep running. They have reason to be concerned if their business' destiny is in the hands of an out-of-control organization! This cycle eventually leads to losing a valuable customer.

As a manager, you are responsible for managing your entire organization, regardless of where they reside. A tough decision you may face is to bring a team member back from a customer site. The customer and the team member may both be unhappy about that decision. It doesn't matter, you will have less damage to deal with by making this tough decision early on. Sometimes, this is a good reminder to the off-site team of how difficult everyone's job is, including that of the central team! Sometimes the off-site teams lose sight of the fact that the central team is always working to provide them the support they need, but all solutions are not easy to deliver. Delays happen and it is the job of the off-site team to put the customer's concerns at rest. When they can no longer do that, it is time to change up the team.

An important job of a manager is put together quotes for the customer. These quotes need to be profitable to the business, while not pricing yourself out of the market. Remember that your customer can go to the competition. They have no obligation to stay with you. Sometimes, earning one dollar per hour profit is better than losing the business, especially if you can keep your competition out in the cold! Make sure you include all expenses, no matter how small, in your price calculation. Before you take on a task of putting together a price quote, you need to meet with your Finance Department to make sure you understand their rules. One area that is off limits to your customer is your internal expense calculations. You should never share this information with your customer as they will question your calculations, questioning the costs of your business. This is confidential information and is not to be shared with anyone outside of your business.

If a customer is willing to share with you their budget, and if you trust that that is really their budget, you should try to line your price up with their budget. I have had many meetings with customers working to get my price in line with their budget. There were always trade-offs. I would remove something from the quote that would lower the price, they would remove a requirement that would also lower the price. You cannot be expected to deliver something for nothing, unless, of course, your manager wants the business no matter what the cost. Once you and your customer come to an agreement and sign on the dotted line, it is important to closely track the budget to ensure you are in line with your plan. You need to record all deviations, along with the reason for the deviation. This information will be valuable for the next price quote you will need to put together. You should never repeat your mistakes!

One important thing to remember, your customers can make or break you! Never underestimate the power of your customers. Never take them for granted. Don't share with them more than necessary to keep the business. Don't divulge your company's secrets to them. Meet your commitments! A delighted customer goes a long way for both your business and for you!

Important Management Points

What is a Mentor?

I have had many mentors over the years. They were all higher than me on the management ladder and they have all helped me through difficult times! These mentors have been my go-to people when I was uncertain about what to do. As I gained more experience at higher levels of management, I have had fewer reasons to call on them for help. However, when I was a more junior manager, they helped me out tremendously, leading to my continuous promotions!

One of my managers nominated me for an official professional women's mentor program in Georgia. This program introduced me to a mentor who helped me work through my first peer problem as a manager. His advice sent me down a path that eventually lead to numerous promotions. He taught me to step back, list possible outcomes based on specific actions, and choose the outcome I preferred. Then, put a plan together to attain the preferred outcome. I followed his advice, ended up leaving the company, taking on a higher management position with a competing company. I realized that the prize was not worth the fight, a valuable management lesson! The manager that nominated me for this program saw potential in me as a manager. While she was my manager, she treated me as a peer. She was able to give me constructive criticism in a way that was truly constructive. I welcomed her feedback on my performance. In fact, I attribute my success as a manager to her. She saw my potential and built on my strengths. She gave me continuous feedback, something I have not received since then.

My other mentor is a true strength in business and management. I still call him when I need help. He always presents to me several options for any particular situation, and explains how he would handle it if it was up to him. He has always been accurate in his assessments.

I have been very fortunate to have access to this wealth of knowledge. It is much easier to do your job when you can learn from someone else's mistakes. No sense in repeating bad history! I reserve my calls to my mentor for those times when I have nowhere else to turn. I know that if I take certain issues to my manager, I will not get the advice I need to succeed. These are the times I call my mentor.

I have also given back as a mentor. I have participated in a couple of official mentor-mentee programs as a mentor. One of the best compliments given to me as a manager is when someone tells me they learned something from me! It makes me happy as a manager to be able to share the things I have learned over the years, hence, this book!

Attitude is Everything

I have hired employees purely based on having the right attitude. When a company is preparing to downsize, those employees with good attitudes and those employees with key skills are the employees who get to keep their jobs. Of course, having the right attitude but no skills to back it up is not too helpful. However, having the right attitude and demonstrating the ability to learn new skills is an excellent combination!

I have interviewed individuals and made hiring decisions based on whether someone has the potential to be successful. Fifty percent of potential is based on the attitude an individual portrays, while the other fifty percent is based on the ability to learn.

Nobody wants to work with someone with a negative attitude. Negativity is viewed as someone who does not hesitate to put a problem on my desk and expect me to find a solution. If I am expected to find solutions to everyone's problems, especially when I feel that the individual asking for the solution should be quite capable of finding that solution himself, I don't need that employee. If I am doing the work of someone who reports to me, why do I need that person? I can say with confidence that I don't!

Delegating

As I had stated previously, a good manager volunteers for more. It is important to note that if you volunteer, you need to be able to deliver! Simply volunteering is not enough. In order to deliver, you need to delegate. In order to delegate, you need a team strong enough to delegate to. Because you volunteered to get the task done, you need to ensure it actually gets done!

Delegating is the act of assigning a task to someone else. Your team may say that they cannot possibly take on any more. You need to sit down with them and help them prioritize their tasks. Many times, your employees spend a lot of time on a trivial task. You need to help them re-prioritize, focusing on those tasks that are the most important for the organization, letting trivial tasks slide. Sometimes, however, they may categorize a particular task as trivial, but you have information that says that the task should actually be a high priority. By reviewing this information with them, you are able to prevent a potential disaster.

While on the topic of priorities, another compliment given to me by a peer is that I am really good at prioritizing. If I have multiple meetings scheduled for the same timeslot, I choose which meeting will get my attention. Many times, it is based purely on politics...who will be in attendance. I will not miss a meeting if I know my manager will be there. Also, I will not miss a meeting if it is called by a customer. If there is a conflict between these two, the customer meeting wins out. Vendor meetings fall to the bottom of the list. Employee meetings fall somewhere in the middle. Also, if there is a meeting called with all of my peers, I will attend. It is important to keep tabs on what they are up to. As part of delegating, I will ask my managers to cover for me if I have a true conflict and need to be at more than one meeting at the same time.

Getting Your Work Done

If I make a commitment, I deliver on the commitment, with no exception. I take on tasks that others are afraid to take on. I have learned to organize my thoughts in a logical way so that I can multitask and get everything done on time. Writing things down helps me with this. I make full use of my whiteboard in my office. Not only does it keep me on track, it shows my management team what the priorities are. I always have the support and respect of the entire organization, my organization along with the organizations of my peers. Whether or not I have the authority to direct other organizations, I take it. As a result, everyone is willing to work with me to get the work done. I work to gain their support. They come to me for advice, no matter what level they are in the organization. I have always maintained my sense of humor. I have fun at work, otherwise, I don't want the job! Because of this, all meetings start with amusing discussions. We all laugh, then we get on with business. We all work as one big team. Those with assignments do not miss deadlines. How is this possible? We meet regularly to track progress. Nobody wants to be embarrassed in front of their peers, therefore, everyone works hard to get the work done. I spend my time delegating the assignments to the appropriate individuals, tracking progress in getting everything completed, and finally compiling the results into a comprehensive solution.

I also help with the work assignments. If someone appears to be underwater and not able to get his tasks completed on time, I will sit down with him to discuss his priorities and his workload. I will then find help for him, either in the way of canceling some of his assignments, or find someone else who can take some of the work off of his plate. Most of the time, someone is waiting on the work of someone else in order to complete her tasks. If that work is delivered late, it impacts the entire project. As a manager, I feel responsible to prevent deadlines from being missed. Therefore, I help the employees so that they can succeed at their work, the project will be delivered on time, and I will not miss a commitment.

In all my years as a manager, I have never had a mutiny. I have been successful in getting everyone to join the team and act as a team. I attribute this success to maintaining a sense of humor, having fun, and being part of the team, versus being the manager of the team. I am always the one with a funny remark during stressful times. Don't get me wrong, I do recognize when it is time to be serious and to buckle down. However, these times are few and far between.

In addition, I insist that my employees maintain a balance between work and life. They know that they should never hesitate to tell me that they have to come in late, leave early, or take time off for family matters! A child's Kindergarten Spring Musical is just as important as a meeting with a customer. In those cases when there is an important meeting that should not be missed, I encourage the employee to find a replacement for the meeting to make sure we have coverage. Also, I am very lenient with comp time. If an employee works all weekend to install a software upgrade, that employee deserves two other days off as a replacement for their weekend. If an employee stays up until 4:00 AM to ensure something goes right, that employee is not expected to be at work at 8:00 AM. While I have never been considered an overly compassionate manager, I have always been considered a fair manager. A team of burnt out, over worked employees is a team of nonproductive, unhappy employees. Each employee must be valued, appreciated, and respected. They deserve their personal time as much as we deserve their work time!

It sounds like a perfect management world, doesn't it? Well, it's not always so easy! I have had to pull rank on occasion, reminding the team that I am the manager and we will do it my way. I reserve this for those times when it is clear to me that I need to step in and take control. I do this when I see that a decision that has been made will be detrimental to the business, and I am not able to convince the team to change their direction. One small example of this is when I was given a challenge of doubling my staff within months with competent, high performing technical resources. I reviewed each and every resume and assigned the best candidates to one of my supervisors to handle the interviews. One of the candidates I passed on was not accepted by the team as a viable candidate. I strongly disagreed, based on my thoughts of this candidate's potential. I overruled the team, insisting that they interview this candidate. They reluctantly agreed that he was qualified and should be offered a position. We hired him. He became one of the highest technical performers throughout the entire organization, continuously promoted. At first my team was not happy with my intervention, however, they finally admitted that it was the right thing to do and that I knew what I was doing!

Make and Meet Commitments

In order to be successful in your career, no matter what your level, it is crucial that you meet all of your commitments! Your customers, your manager, your peers, and your team all need to know they can count on you! If you say you are going to do something, you need to do it. I realize that this is not always possible. In those cases where you simply cannot get it done, you need to communicate early and communicate often. You never want to surprise anyone on a due date with the fact that you didn't do it. It doesn't matter who you made that commitment to, if you make a commitment you need to meet it!

One of the keys to my success is my ability to meet commitments. Everyone knows they can count on me! Sometimes this requires that I find creative solutions to problems, especially in those cases where the task seems impossible. My ability to step back from a situation, ponder the options, and devise a plan leading to a solution has lead to every one of my career successes! Sometimes, taking a break from a situation puts your mind at ease and allows you to think clearer about the problem. I laugh when I think of how many solutions I have come up with while in the shower! If the problem you are working on appears too large to solve, break it down into smaller problems. This will make it more manageable. You will then be able to solve each smaller problem, leading to a solution for the big problem. You will hear people say "chunk it down." They are referring to this process of breaking something down into smaller parts, dealing with the smaller parts, eventually leading to an overall solution. This process will help you delegate different parts of the problem to different individuals, versus giving one big problem to one person to solve. It is a productive way to handle a large issue without overwhelming someone with what could seem to be an impossible task.

Many commitments require the assistance of your management team and/or your team members. The only way you can meet these commitments is if you have their unconditional support, as some of these commitments require substantial time and resource commitments. However, I will not make that commitment if I didn't believe it was deliverable. For these larger initiatives, I pull the team together, explain the reason for the commitment, explain the preferred outcome, and then start taking their ideas on how we can accomplish it. Getting the team's buy-in helps ensure they will support the plan and do whatever it takes to get the work done.

I have had many direct report managers remind me that a particular commitment is not my job, rather, it is the job of one of my peers. I quickly point out that it is something that should have been done a long time ago and it appears that my peer does not have the wherewithal to get it done. This is one of those times when I get to rise above my peers and contribute to the overall success of the business. When I see a shortcoming, something that needs attention but it's not getting the attention it needs, I always step in and take it over. This is sometimes frustrating to my team as they feel I get them involved in things they don't have time for, things they are not really responsible for. Regardless, they still jump in and help make it a success. Not because they want the additional work, but because I am able to educate them in the importance of the task to the success of the business. Sometimes, I take on these tasks simply for political reasons. If I know that my manager wants something done because he committed to his manager, I will be the first to step up and take it. This puts me in favor with my manager, and puts my manager in favor with his manager. There is never anything wrong with getting positive recognition at all levels of management! Taking on a task for political reasons is even more frustrating to my teams. I am still able to explain the benefit of completing the task to the organization and get them on board.

While it may appear that I bite off more than I can chew, I never take on something I don't believe can be successfully completed. Some things may fall to the bottom of the list of priorities, however, it is comforting to management to know that someone has it on their list. At times, the priority list needs to be shuffled and things on the bottom move up to the top. This is all part of the need to be flexible as a manager. It is not possible to add hours to a day, but it is possible to decide the best way to use those hours available to you. Sometimes something you have been working on diligently gets canceled. You need to shrug your shoulders and move on to the next task. This happens every day in business and it is important to remain flexible in order to handle these constant changes.

Don't Put it in Writing

Whatever you do, don't put anything in writing that you will regret later. Sometimes, you may feel so frustrated that you sit down and draft an email, an email that will get you into trouble.

First of all, don't ever put a "To:" address in the email until you are certain you are going to send it, as, sometimes, tapping your mouse may cause it be sent.

Secondly, read and reread your email to make sure you are okay with the content. This pertains to every email you are writing, regardless of who you are sending it to. Check for content, make sure your email is saying what you want it to say. Check for grammar and spelling mistakes. Nothing is more irritating to me then to receive an email riddled with grammar and spelling mistakes! It tells me that the person sending the email doesn't care about the impression they leave. If this is the case, I must conclude that this person does his job with the same attitude.

One caveat to this is to be sensitive to the fact that the email may be coming from a non-native English speaker. In this case, I am always in awe over their master of the English language, knowing how difficult it is to learn to speak, read, and write a second language, especially to the extent of being able to conduct business in that language!

Back to the reason for this topic. Some people feel brave behind a keyboard. They will put their emotions into an email and send it. I always save those emails as evidence that there may be a problem with the individual sending them. I am always very guarded about what I say and what I write. I never speak out or write with emotion. I always remain calm and collected, no matter what the situation. People will always remember what you say or write, especially if it is inappropriate. Emails can be forwarded to your manager or to HR for personnel action. Emails can also be used in the case of a legal investigation. Therefore, if you put it in writing, it becomes a permanent record on your behalf. As a result, make sure that you have a positive permanent record, or you are willing to deal with the repercussions of sending the email.

Remember that if you are not brave enough to say it, you shouldn't be brave enough to write it. If you put it in writing, chances are, you'll be confronted about it, possibly in a face-to-face encounter, which means you are going to have to defend your position. When this happens, you are going to have to say it. So, if you're not brave enough to say it, don't be brave enough to write it!

If you get pulled into an email war, employees sending accusatory, aggressive emails back and forth, it is your job to put an end to it. Sometimes this requires calling a face-to-face meeting with the participants. Other times it requires sending an email to the entire distribution list putting an end to the messages. Email wars usually start due to an accusation being made by the originator. The recipient always feels the need to respond. The distribution list grows with every reply. Sooner or later, you will be copied. When this happens, it is time to intervene and put an end to it. As a manager, you need to determine the reason for the emails and help resolve the issue. When having to intervene more than once, I have gone as far as making a rule that no more emails could be sent. If an issue needed to be discussed, the originator was told to pick up the phone and call the individual, or, better yet, walk over to his office for a face-to-face discussion. This approach has always worked.

Social Media

Social media is something to be addressed in today's work environments. Policies need to be defined around the use of social media as it is something that is prominent in social collaboration. Employees use social media to stay in touch with friends, families, and colleagues. The use of social media is a distracting force in the office. If rules are placed around the use of social media, and employees are made aware of its use, a happy medium can be struck between employers and employees.

As a manager, it is important to remind those employees under you that whatever is published via social media can never be erased. Once it is out there, it is out there to stay. We have seen beauty queens lose their titles as a result of something published ten years ago. We have seen employees fired as a result of something published two days ago. While it may seem like you are about to publish something harmless on a social media site, remember that the definition of harmless is in the eye of the beholder. In other words, every individual has a different opinion of what harmless means. Making an assumption about something you deem harmless could be a career limiting move. My advice is if you are in doubt, don't write it! Is it something worth losing your job over (either now or in the future)? Ask yourself this question every time you get the urge to post something.

Don't Ignore History

This is especially important for taking on a new management role. You need to understand the history of how the organization got to where it is. You don't want to repeat bad history! If something had been tried previously, but didn't work, you need to understand why it didn't work. If circumstances have changed since that failed attempt, it may be okay to try it again. If, however, circumstances have stayed the same, you need to come up with a new approach.

You never want to make the same mistake twice, even if the first mistake was due to someone else's efforts.

One new manager, a peer, started a position in a very aggressive way. He continuously said he didn't care about the history, that we were taking on a fresh start. Well, that attitude didn't work so well. He made a decision to take an action that had been tried previously. It failed the first time, and it failed the second time. After doing this a couple of times, he was out. He lasted only three weeks! Watching him taught me a valuable lesson – don't ever ignore history!

As a result of this lesson, I always start a new job observing rather than doing. I try not to make any major changes until I have been on the job for a few months. I observe, I listen, I question, but I don't change, unless there are glaring needs for change. One job I took on required that I take personnel action immediately. My manager gave me a head's up that this was probably needed, but he wanted me to come to the same conclusion on my own. It took me one day to realize that I had to take action quickly, action that should had been taken years before, but the previous manager decided it was easier to ignore the problem than it was to fix the problem. This was one of those instances when I had to break my own rule and take action sooner rather than later. Sometimes the issue is so obvious, it is okay to act quickly and make a change. This should be the exception, however, not the norm.

Always start a new job learning first, implementing change second. Understand the history, understand the politics, understand the organization, then look for improvement opportunities. Change for the sake of change is a wasted energy.

Change is Good

Remember that change is good. Whether change is in the form of a reorganization, a new manager, losing a key employee, moving to a new office, taking on new responsibilities, moving to a new company, whatever the change may be, it is important to look at each change as a new, exciting challenge. I enjoy change. It prevents you from getting into a rut, doing the same thing day-in and day-out, getting bored with your job! It is rewarding to rise from change as a success. Flexibility is a very important characteristic of a good manager. This means that you must be receptive to change. It should not derail you or your organization. Proper planning will help you survive any change. Take the time to put together a plan, no matter how small the change. Surprises are bad, plans are good! Prepare for every outcome and you will succeed. Your manager will be relieved when you willingly accept change. Many managers fret over announcing changes, due to the fact that many members of their team are resistant to change.

It is important to include your management team in planning for change.

Your manager will want to see that you are comfortable with change. He does not want to hear complaints, rather ideas on how to make it successful. Many times, your manager is not happy about the change, however, he has been directed to take action and is passing it on to his staff. It is important that you embrace the change and work to make it successful.

As a manager, you are also responsible for getting your staff to understand and accept changes. Those employees who fall towards to the bottom of the totem pole aren't always as accepting of change as your management team. If this is case, you and your management team need to work a little harder to get everyone on board. Hold an organizational communication meeting to explain the change to everyone. Let them all hear the same story at the same time. Give them a chance to ask questions and voice concerns. This will be your opportunity to get everyone on board and supportive of the coming change. Sometimes you need to remind them that like it or not, the change is coming. They can either get on board and help make it a success, or find a job elsewhere (assuming they feel that strongly against it).

Balance

You need to maintain a healthy balance between work and personal life. Time off may be difficult to schedule due to your workload, however, downtime helps you do your job better. When you take time off, you need to disconnect from your job. The only work related calls you should take are *real* emergencies, not simply updates about what's going on around the office. Your family and friends deserve your undivided attention. It is also your job to insist the same of your staff. They need to take the time off to refresh as well. In addition, if they need to arrive late due to a family commitment, or leave early, it is your job to be supportive of this. The work will always get done! There needs to be, however, a balance between time off and time on the job. If an employee appears to be taking advantage of your "balanced life" philosophy, you need to address it before it becomes a problem. What is normal? The answer is "it depends." Some employees, those who work twice as hard as all others, those willing to give up nights and weekends when needed, may deserve extra personal time, while others, those who are always late and always leaving early, taking an unusually high number of sick days, may not deserve your leniency.

The one thing I always hated my manager to say to me was "just make sure your work gets done." It was never necessary for any manager to say this to me. I take personal offense to this statement. In fact, as I became more experienced as a manager, I haven't heard this comment in a long time. It is important to show your manager in advance that you have a good handle on your workload before asking for time off. Beat your manager to the punch, don't give him the opportunity to make such a comment to you. Be proactive in giving them a status on all outstanding assignments.

Regular weekly status reports to your manager will keep him up-to-date on what you and your organization are up to. If your manager does not have an official template for such a report, make one up. Send him a report each week, whether he asks for it or not. You need him to know that you are getting the work done, that your organization is busy working on the right things, and that your customers are being taken care of.

Diversity

Diversity is the way of life. It cannot be ignored. In fact, it needs to be understood and respected. Every different background contributes something different and valuable. Brainstorming sessions, sessions where all ideas are put on the table, no matter how different the idea may seem, and then each idea is discussed by the group and considered as a viable idea, are valuable tools used to find creative solutions. Diversity leads to a wide variety of ideas being put on the table. The more ideas put on the table, the more ideas to consider when searching for solutions.

The Merriam-Webster definition of Diversity is:

The condition of being <u>diverse</u> : VARIETY;
especially : **the inclusion of** <u>diverse</u> **people (as
people of different races or cultures) in a group or
organization <programs intended to promote
diversity in schools>** [4]

If you find yourself working for a company headquartered in
another country (outside of the United States), it is important
to learn about the culture and the work habits of that culture.
In order to succeed in this type of environment, you need to
understand why your colleagues make the decisions they
make as well as how to work with them in the most
productive way. If you are working in an international
location, you should make an effort to learn the language,
learn the culture, and learn the local traditions. You need to
participate as a local versus watch as an outsider. You also
need to familiarize yourself with the employment laws of that
country. Breaking the employment law in a foreign country
could be extremely costly to your company, and, possibly,
risky for you personally.

If you are managing a diverse team in the United States, you need to be sensitive to the various cultures, however, you should not have different performance expectations across the various cultures. No matter where the employee is from, no matter what the background of the employee is, each employee is expected to deliver. If you are managing employees from different countries, and you are located in the United States, each employee is expected to behave according to the employment laws of the United States. You are responsible for ensuring the laws are followed, that harassment or discrimination are never accepted in your organization, or anywhere else within the business.

If you are working for a U.S. company, it should be expected that all employees have a good command of the English language, regardless of where the office is located. If you are working for a U.S. based company in a foreign country, and the company's policy is that all business will be conducted in the English language, it is your job to enforce this policy. All

meetings should be conducted in English. It is important

that this policy be enforced, due to the fact that those

employees who do not speak the local language can easily

misinterpret comments being made in that language, leading

to a very non-productive environment.

Show Your Knowledge

You need to present your knowledge and progress at every opportunity given to you. You need to be well versed in the use of presentation creation software. Your presentations should be succinct, accurate, and thorough. Determine the level of detail based on who the audience is. If you are presenting a work plan to your team, you need to present significant detail. The higher level the employees in your audience, the less detail should be included. Executive management will sit through a summary and will want to see sufficient detail to show you are on top of things. They do not have the attention span, nor the time, to sit through long, detailed presentations, unless they specifically ask for such a thing. If you see their eyes gloss over, you just stepped over that line into too much detail.

Your manager will want to know who the owners of tasks are and the estimated completion dates. Include this level of detail, but keep it at that, unless otherwise requested.

You should look for opportunities to present at professional conferences. These presentations are usually based on "Lessons Learned." The goal of these presentations is to teach your colleagues how to get something done efficiently, new ways of doing things, new ways to organize, etc. You should use these opportunities to gain positive recognition for your company. You want to show successes, not failures. It is okay to show how something that you tried failed, however, you should only do this if you follow it up with another idea that succeeded. Presenting at professional conferences will lead you to becoming known in industry. The more contacts you have, the more people can help you when you need something. Making contacts can help you in your current job, they can help you find a new job, they can share with you their experiences, etc.

You should write articles for your company's newsletter. This is another way to gain visibility for you and your team. You should not, however, be part of the social committee. You should find a volunteer in your organization to participate, however, you have more important things to tend to then to plan the next holiday party.

Agree With Your Boss

Arguing with your manager is a career limiting move. Remember that your manager decides your destiny. In fact, if you decide to argue with your manager, you have taken your destiny into your own hands, not necessarily with an outcome you were hoping for. If you disagree with your manager, bring it to his attention in private, not in a public forum. Always show support for your manager and his ideas in

public. It is my opinion that it is okay to be a "yes person."
Agree with your boss, say "yes" to his ideas, then go back to
your office and figure out how you're going to get it done.
Throughout my career, my success has been the result of
having a supportive manager. I have had supportive
managers because I am supportive of them.

Instead of telling my manager that I disagree with her idea, I
raise some additional things to consider that maybe weren't
taken into account. This could sway her to change her plan.
If, however, after raising these concerns, she still wants to go
forward with her plan, remember that she is your manager for
a reason and it is your job to help her succeed (assuming
there is nothing morally or ethically wrong with her plan).

I have always been the manager that my manager goes to for
help. Mainly because I am in agreement with their plans and
help them carry them out. I haven't ever argued with my

manager. I haven't ever told my manager "No." Instead, I work to clearly understand their thoughts so that I can contribute to their solution. I am always able to deliver something to my manager based on his request. I never immediately commit a solution. Rather, I take the request back to my office where I think about the possible solutions and plan an approach. I usually involve my management team in this thought process as they will most likely be involved in delivery of the solution. I take work off of my manager's plate versus put it on. I do this for a couple of reasons: First, I like to be considered the go-to person by my manager; second, the more I learn about the organization, the easier it will be to take over the organization some day. My goal in my career has always been to take on more responsibility, either by increasing the size of my organization, taking on the management of additional teams, or even taking over my manager's job, all of which I have done at some point in time in my career.

I never take a problem to my manager without a list of alternative solutions. If I handed all of my problems over to my manager, why would she need me? In fact, I expect the same of my entire organization. If someone brings a problem into my office, they need to bring alternative solutions. We will then discuss the options and figure out together the best way to proceed. Sometimes, however, an employee has no solution and he can't figure out where to even begin. This does happen. Under these circumstances, we will sit down and work through it together. This is an exception, however, not a norm.

I am, in fact, a "Yes person." In my opinion, nothing is impossible, given the time to figure it out. Therefore, when my manager comes to me and asks me to take care of something, my immediate response is "Yes, I've got it." When I say those words, my manager knows that I can be counted on to get it taken care of. As a result, I am the person my manager will go to in order to get things done. This is really important when you are trying to become an insider and someone your manager is comfortable confiding in. The more knowledge you gain from an insider perspective, the better you can do your job. The better you do your job, the better jobs will be given to you!

Politics

Politics is something nobody talks about. You don't learn about politics in your college text books. Politics exist in everything you do in business. In fact, it doesn't matter what the industry is, politics run rampant throughout the organization. Who should you align yourself with, who is in the inner circle, who is a cast out, who do you want to form an alliance with, who should you avoid, the list goes on and on. Some decisions you make will be based purely on politics. You may take on an assignment simply due to who is making the request. If you can get recognition by your manager's manager, you may want to take on the task. If you want to keep your manager out of trouble with his manager, you may want to take on the task.

No matter what your level is in an organization, you cannot ignore politics. You will hear some people say they will not get involved in the politics of the business. This is a career limiting move. You need to be able to scheme like the best of them. You need to analyze every problem, both for the business impact and for the political impact. If you have heard a rumor that somebody is going to be given the assignment of "special projects," you need to steer clear of that person. That person has been tagged as a "loser" and your association with that person puts you in the "loser" category as well. While this sounds harsh, it is a reality. If you are part of the inner circle, people will want to align themselves with you, whether they like you or not. Remember that you are not here to make friends. You are here to further your career and help make the business successful. Don't confuse respect for friendship. You don't need your colleagues to like you, but you do need them to respect you!

The political situation dictates how free or how guarded you need to be with your comments. Speaking up may not be the best policy. In fact, sitting back and being quiet may be your best bet. Always listen to what is being said, then follow up later if you have concerns. While you may be tempted to corner someone, there are times when this is okay, and times when this should be avoided. You can always follow up and voice your opinions later, however, if you speak up at the wrong time, it is too late, the harm has been done. It is okay to ask questions, however, these questions should not appear controversial, rather, they should appear as clarifying, especially in a group setting. You never want to appear as not being on board. You never want to appear negative. There are positive ways to say anything. You can deliver the worst news in a positive way. Always emphasize the good while presenting the bad.

Another important part of politics is figuring out who to be aligned with and who to avoid. If your manager has a "favorite" direct report, you need to figure out who that person is and why they are his favorite. Watch how that person interacts with your manager. You will probably notice that she always agrees with your manager, no matter what. You will probably notice that all "visible" assignments go to this peer. Your goal should be to, at a minimum, be viewed in the same light by your manager, or, preferably, to take over that person's position. Many times, it is hard to step into your peer's role, as there is history between her and your manager. Once a manager decides who to trust, that trust is rarely broken. You can make progress in gaining the same level of trust by taking on tasks that are not directly related to your job, tasks that span the entire organization. You then need to deliver! Missing such a commitment will be devastating to your career at that company. Most of these tasks are highly visible, and sometimes requested by your manager's manager. While performing these tasks, you need to frequently communicate status to your manager. He needs to know that you have made this your priority and are making progress in getting it completed. If you hit a roadblock, it is crucial to communicate this as soon as is practical. Take a small amount of time to try to overcome the roadblock. Your goal should be to find a solution to the roadblock on your own. If, however, you are running out of time and just cannot find a way around the roadblock, you need to communicate to your manager so he is not surprised if you miss a key deadline.

It is a good idea to do simple things like going to lunch with the trusted peer. If this peer believes you are doing a good job, she will put in some good words for you to your manager. This peer can make or break you, given the trust your manager has placed in her. She is usually chosen as your boss' delegate when he is out of the office. She is probably in line to take your manager's job if and when he moves on. Your goal is to be considered equal to her, or better than her.

In addition to dealing with your peers, you need to gain visibility with your manager's manager. Usually, this happens by your manager having enough confidence in you to help you gain this visibility. If your manager feels that you are supportive of her and her ideas, she will have the confidence to get you face-to-face time with her manager. If, on the other hand, she is afraid that you may use a meeting with her manager as a self-promotion opportunity, possibly complaining to her manager about her performance, she will prevent you from having that meeting. If your manager's

manager is aware of your abilities, he will request your

involvement when appropriate. If he doesn't know you exist,

those prime assignments will go to your peers. Therefore, it

is in your best interest to watch for an opportunity to get

invited to a meeting with your manager's manager, prepare

appropriately for the meeting, and make your manager proud.

Managing Your Destiny

How to Get Hired

Your resume is your first introduction to a potential employer. It is important to ensure that your resume is succinct and highlights your major accomplishments. Make sure your resume shows your broad span of experience. I was always taught that a resume should only be one page long. I have not found this practical. I cannot fit my experiences on a one-page resume. I can barely fit my education and my certifications on one page, let alone my work history! I have never refused to interview a candidate due to having a resume longer than one page!

Good managers need to be process oriented, looking for continuous improvement opportunities, supportive of diversity, knowledgeable of the industry, knowledgeable of quality, and willing to do whatever it takes to get the job done. All of these topics need to be touched on in an interview. I have learned over the years that processes are lacking just about everywhere. Organizations need processes in order to repeat successes. In addition, organizations need an injection of quality. Knowledge of quality is also valuable. Being able to speak to quality improvement is valuable in an interview. Every industry has quality associated with it. Software development values SEI CMM, ITIL, etc. It is important to understand the various quality processes valued in your industry and to be able to explain your knowledge in these processes and how you have applied them to improve quality. Another characteristic I have found valuable to potential employers is the willingness of a candidate to take on difficult personnel issues. This refers back to "How to Deal With Bad Employees." Many managers are afraid to take necessary personnel action to clean up a nonproductive organization. Your ability to show evidence of how you have handled such a situation in the past will win you points in your interview. Another important area to cover in an interview is your ability to multitask. It is important to be able to juggle many balls without letting any one of them fall. Flexibility is another key area. Employers are looking for managers who are flexible, managers who don't get frustrated with a constant shift in priorities.

It is important to show confidence in an interview without appearing arrogant or cocky. I have been offered every job I have ever interviewed for. This is due to being properly qualified for each position, as well as being prepared for the interview. I have learned to interview the hiring employer at the same time as being interviewed. I made one mistake in my career, accepting a position that was neither well defined, nor looked at as a valuable position within the business. As a result, I was extremely unhappy, trying to do something that was not viewed as necessary to the business. Because of this mistake, I learned to ask many questions about the job to make sure it is something that would make me happy. Given that a person spends nearly ten hours per day in the office, it is important to be happy at your job! My advice is to not accept a position just because the money is good. Being miserable at a job ten or more hours per day is not worth any amount of money being offered!

Proper preparation for an interview includes assembling a list of your accomplishments throughout your career. This list is for your reference when being interviewed. When in an interview situation, you may become nervous and you will probably forget some of your important accomplishments that may be related to the job you are applying for. By assembling a list of these accomplishments, you will be certain to point out the important points of your background, leading to being offered the job. I always walk out of an interview wishing I would have said this or that, however, being prepared in advance lessens these concerns.

During the interview, take your time to answer the questions. Don't feel the need to jump right in and answer immediately. Think before you speak. Prepare your answer in your head before answering your interviewer. Preparing in advance of the interview will assist you with being able to answer the questions posed of you.

Make sure to dress appropriately for the interview. If the company that is interviewing you has a casual dress policy, you should still wear a suit, regardless of your gender. You could make it a bit more casual upon your arrival for the interview by simply taking off your jacket. However, I would only do this if my interviewer made the suggestion. Otherwise, keep your jacket on, make sure your clothes are properly cleaned and ironed, make sure your shoes are freshly polished, and make sure that everything matches.

During the interview, get business cards from each person interviewing you. As soon as you arrive home, immediately following the interview, send thank you emails to each person you spoke with. Customize each email for each recipient. In each email, refer to a certain quality or qualification you have that makes you the best candidate for the job.

When you get the job, you need to dress like your manager, assuming you are after your manager's job. If the dress policy calls for business casual attire, you need to not follow this policy when meeting with customers or more senior managers. For these times you need to dress like you are going on an interview. People will judge you on first impressions, and the very first impression is how you are dressed. They will notice your attire before you ever have a chance to greet them.

How to Get Fired

I have provided many thoughts on how not to manage throughout this book. Each one of those points is an opportunity to be fired. Once you move up into management, the tolerance for mistakes goes down. Sometimes you will only get one strike. Therefore, don't make the mistakes I have explained throughout this book and you'll end up in a rewarding management career. Make any of these mistakes and you could end up on the street looking for another job.

Don't do your job, don't make your customers happy, don't treat your employees fairly, don't treat your colleagues with respect, argue with your manager, break HR laws, overspend your budget, all of these will get you at the least demoted and at the worst fired.

How to Get Promoted

Always go above and beyond. Plan your work and get your work done. Play politics. Deliver quality. Make your customers happy. Help your manager succeed. Take on the difficult tasks and get them done with the highest quality. Treat your employees fairly, include them in your planning. Align yourself with the key members of the team and avoid the under performers. Deliver, deliver, deliver! Make commitments and meet those commitments. Be organized and manage your time wisely. Continuously look for opportunities to improve. Continue with your education. Get another degree, get professionally certified, take courses, attend professional conferences. Broadcast your successes. Over communicate with your manager so he knows the progress you are making. Do all of this and you will get promoted! Do all of this and you will be considered an excellent manager. Do all of this and you will be able to name your price, name your employer, and define your job!

Footnotes

[1]"management." <u>Merriam-Webster Online Dictionary</u>. 2010., Merriam-Webster Online. 4 January 2010, http://www.merriam-webster.com/dictionary/management

[2] "management." Businessdictionary.com, 2010.,

4 January 2010, http://www.businessdictionary.com/

definition/management.html

[3] "customer." <u>Merriam-Webster Online Dictionary</u>. 2010. Merriam-Webster Online. 19 January 2010 http://www.merriam-webster.com/dictionary/customer

[4]"diversity." Merriam-Webster Online Dictionary. 2010. Merriam-Webster Online. 19 January 2010, http://www.merriam-webster.com/dictionary/diversity